I can make things for Easter

Crafts by Jocelyn Miller
Photography by John Williams
Illustration by Adrian Barclay

Contents

LION
CHILDREN'S

1 Springtime leaves

In winter, branches are bare. In spring, their buds burst into leaf. This season echoes the Easter message of new life where all was dead.

Make your own Easter display with bare branches hung with leaves, and ribbon bows like blossom.

1 To make the leaves, fold a strip of paper in half lengthways. Draw a half leaf shape along the crease and cut out. Cut leaves in different sizes.

2 Unfold each leaf and punch a hole at the stem end.

3 Gather up 3 or 4 leaves and thread them onto a ribbon. Tie with a single loose knot. Then tie each cluster onto bare branches arranged in a vase.

If you wish, cut coloured heart shapes to include with some of the bunches.

2 A gift from the heart

This heart-shaped bag is perfect for giving small gifts such as sweets or chocolate.

You could use the same design for a Mothering Sunday gift.

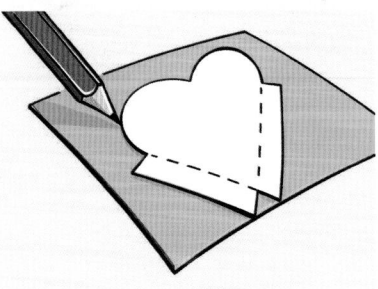

1 Copy the heart template on the back cover and cut it out. Draw around it twice on your choice of thin card and cut out two shapes.

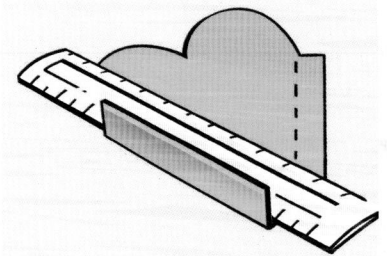

2 Fold up the tab on each piece, using a ruler to get a good straight line. Crease.

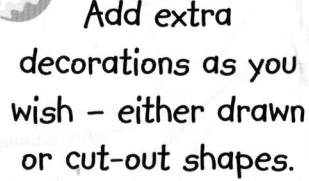

Add extra decorations as you wish – either drawn or cut-out shapes.

3 Put double-sided tape on the outer side of both tabs on one piece. Unpeel the covering and press the tabs of the other piece on top.

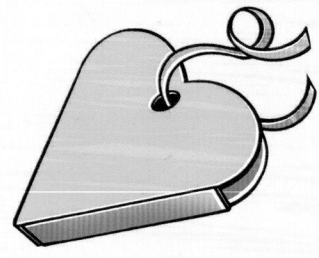

4 Punch a hole through both pieces. When you have filled the bag, thread a ribbon through both holes and tie shut.

3 Easter table

Brighten up your Easter table with these jolly decorations.
Choose a colour theme or even a rainbow of pastel colours.
Water-based emulsion and acrylic paints are the easiest for this.

You can tuck an Easter gift of tiny eggs or sweets into each pot, and hide them with shredded tissue paper.

Grandad

Jack

1 Paint your spoons and terracotta flowerpots with gesso. When they are dry (very soon!), paint a spoon and a pot in each of your colours. Leave to dry.

2 Decorate the spoon with a marker pen. Write on a name if you wish. Tie the ribbon in a bow around as shown.

3 To hold the spoon upright, either use a lump of modelling clay or a handful of washed pebbles in the base of each pot.

4 Easter garden

The story at the heart of Easter is about Jesus. He preached a message of love and forgiveness, but enemies conspired for him to be crucified. Three days later, the Bible says, his friends saw him alive again.

Christians believe that Jesus' new life, his resurrection, is a promise that God's love and forgiveness is for ever.

This Easter garden is a traditional Christian craft, depicting the place where Jesus was buried and the stone door of the tomb rolled away… to reveal that it is empty.

This project takes a few weeks to grow!

1 Choose a large tray for the base. A terracotta saucer for large flowerpots is suitable. Choose a small flowerpot to make the "tomb".

2 Then mix grass seed into potting compost. Make a soil bag from loose-weave fabric, garden hessian, or an old pair of tights! Add soil mix.

3 Put the bag on the tray, patting and shaping into a mound and making sure the pot "tomb" remains just visible. Find a sheltered place outdoors where your garden can grow. Water the soil, and keep it watered.

4 The grass will grow! For Easter itself, make a twig cross tied with raffia for the top. Push that into the top of your garden's green hill. Find a smooth, round stone to be the open door of the tomb.

For display on Easter Sunday, twine ivy around your garden. Push leafy twigs and blossom into the damp soil.

5 Flower and butterfly card

Make this 3D card for someone special this Easter. It is easiest to make your card quite big so the cut-outs aren't too fiddly. Take A4 card and fold it in half.

1 Use the templates on the back cover to cut out the butterfly and petal shapes. Cut a thin notch out of each petal, as marked. Cut a coin–sized circle of thin card for the centre.

2 Make the flower. Taking each petal in turn, overlap the two sides of the notch so the petal curls up and tape in place.

3 When all the petals are in place, glue the circle in the centre.

4 Make the butterfly: First add patterning, stickers, or gemstones to the wings.

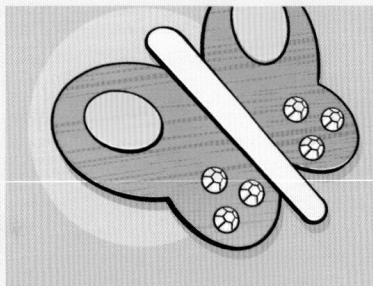

5 Next cut a narrow strip for the body so a "head" and "tail" extend beyond the join in the wings. Lightly glue the body onto the wings.

6 Put glue on the head and tail of the butterfly so you can stick ths strip in place with the wings free to flap.

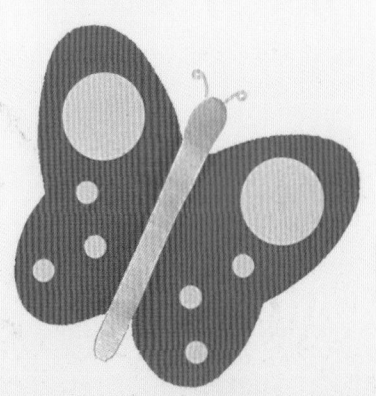

Add a stem
and leaves
for your
flowers if
you wish.

6 Gingerbread Eggs-travaganza

Have fun making these cookies and decorating them extravagantly. If you are having friends or relatives around for Easter, why not have a decorating party!

   Wash your hands before you do any cooking. Ask a grown-up to help, and let them deal with the oven and its controls.

Tie a ribbon around your cookies for a traditional "Easter egg" look.

1 In a bowl put 100g caster sugar, 100g butter, 1 tablespoon of water, 1 tablespoon of black treacle, and 2 tablespoons of golden syrup. Ask a grown-up to melt the ingredients in a microwave. Stir.

2 In a larger bowl mix 250g flour, 1 teaspoon of baking soda, 1 teaspoon of ground ginger, and 1 teaspoon of cinnamon. Add the melted ingredients and mix to form a soft dough. Chill for about 30 minutes.

3 Roll out the dough on baking parchment dusted with flour and cut out egg shapes with a cutter. Lay each gently on a baking tray lined with parchment.

4 Bake for 10 minutes at 160°C. Ask a grown-up to preheat the oven and to lift the cookies in and out. When they are cool, decorate with writing icing and tiny sweets.

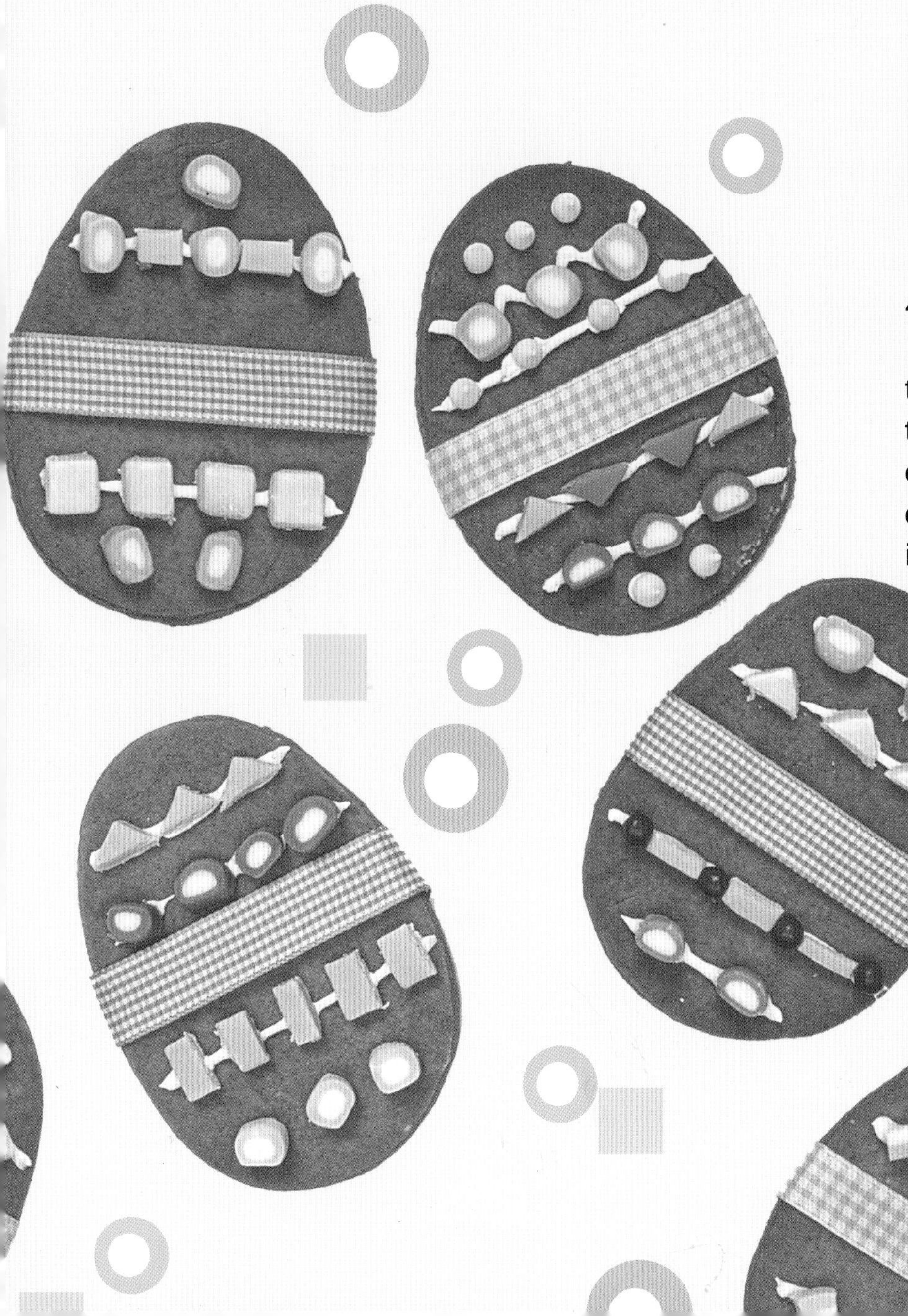

7 Bunny bags

These are fabulous for collecting up your Easter goodies… or taking a gift to a friend.

You could make these with plain brown or white-paper lunch bags, or make your own bag as described here.

1 Take a rectangle of paper or card, 30cm x 45cm (or A3). Fold it as shown to make the body of the bag. Crease the sides and tape the join.

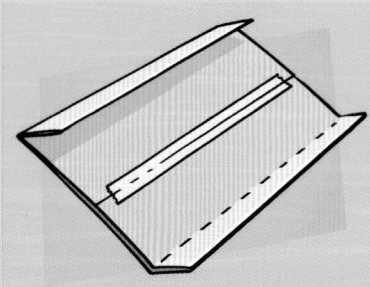

2 Lightly rule a line 3cm in from the crease down each side. Fold, crease, and unfold.

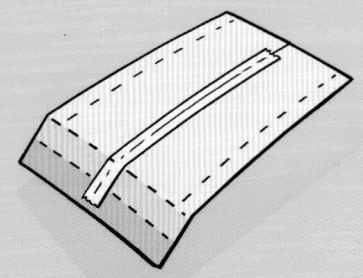

3 Now rule a line 3cm up from the lower edge and another 3cm up from that. Fold, crease, and unfold.

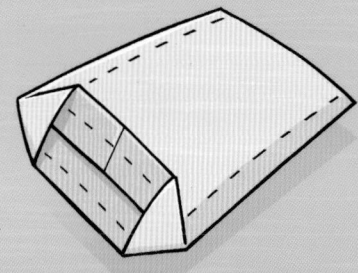

4 Open up the base along the inner crease and squash the corners flat as shown.

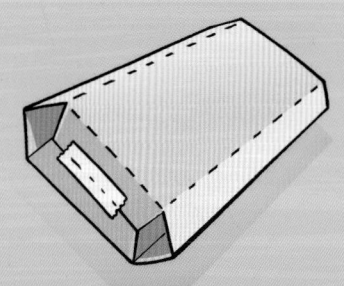

5 Now fold the other two sides in along the crease marks as shown so they just overlap. Tape.

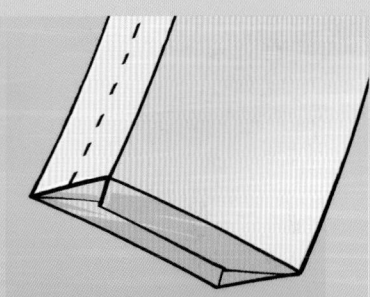

6 Open up the bag and refold the side creases so the pleats go inwards. Squash the bag flat from inside.

Tape cord or ribbon on the inside of the ears, front and back, to make a carrying handle if you wish.

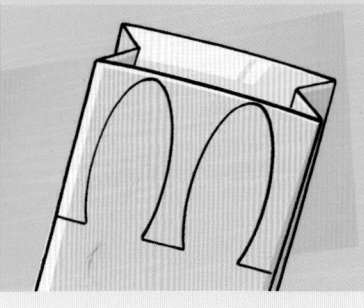

7 Draw your bunny ears and cut out through all thicknesses.

8 Add the inner ears and face with markers.

8 Egg cosy bunny

You could make a small bunny to sit over a boiled egg in a cup. The bunny here, however, is guarding a chocolate egg nestled in a cup cut from a drinks bottle.

Ask a grown-up to help you snip the bottom half of a drinks bottle and nestle a chocolate egg on a tissue-paper nest to put under your rabbit.

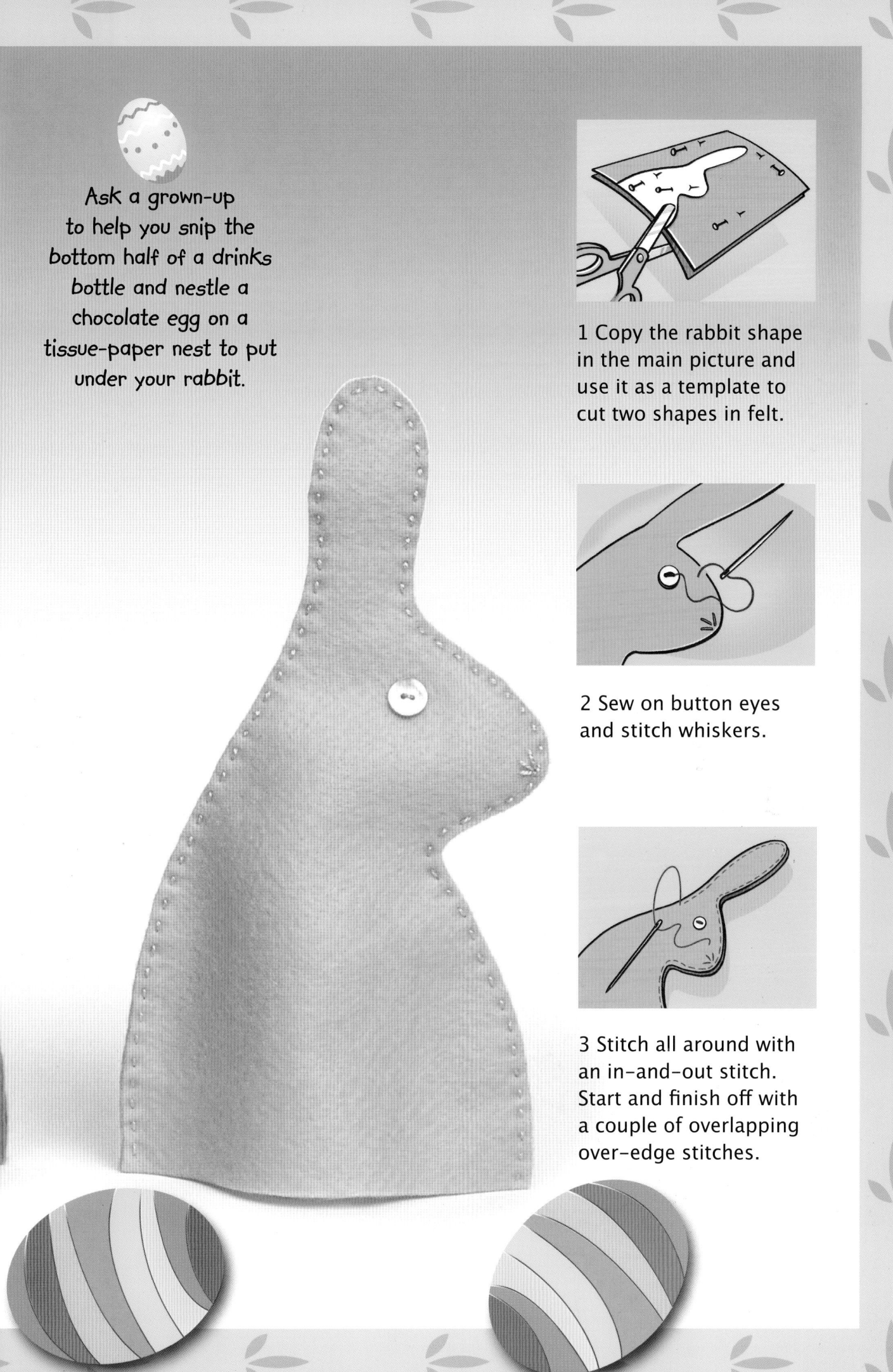

1 Copy the rabbit shape in the main picture and use it as a template to cut two shapes in felt.

2 Sew on button eyes and stitch whiskers.

3 Stitch all around with an in-and-out stitch. Start and finish off with a couple of overlapping over-edge stitches.

9 Dove among the olives

The Bible story of Jesus says that he was buried in a tomb in an olive grove. It was there that a friend, Mary, first saw him alive again.

This hanging wreath for Easter features olive leaves and a dove: traditional symbols of peace.

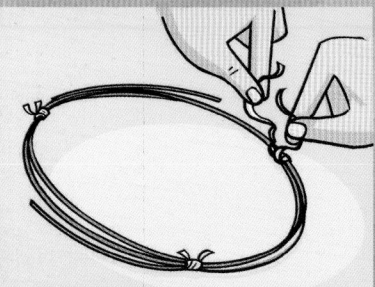

1 Cut long bendy twigs from a tree such as willow or birch and tie them together tightly with raffia to make a circle about 30cm in diameter. Or ask a grown-up to bend wire into a wreath shape.

2 Cut strips of grey and green paper and fold them in half lengthways. Use the template on the back cover to cut leaves the size of olive leaves, with a "stalk".

3 Gather leaves into bunches, using masking tape to cover the stalk.

4 Tie bunches onto the wreath with raffia as shown.

5 Copy the shape in the main picture and use it to cut a bird shape from white card. Add details and attach with a hanging thread.

10 Count your chickens

These cheerful cardboard chickens are designed to be pegged into the ground… a great way to mark out an Easter egg hunt in the garden.

Make your hens quite big so they are easy to see.

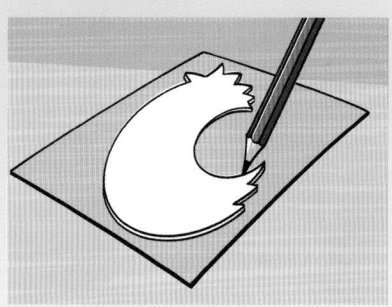  

1 Draw chicken shapes like the ones shown here. Once you have shapes you like, cut them out, and draw around them on cardboard.

2 Cut out your cardboard shapes and paint them with gesso on both sides. Leave to dry, and then press the shapes flat under heavy books or magazines.

3 Paint one side in a plain, bright colour and leave to dry. Then paint the other side and add dots and spots as well as an eye, beak, comb, and tail feathers.

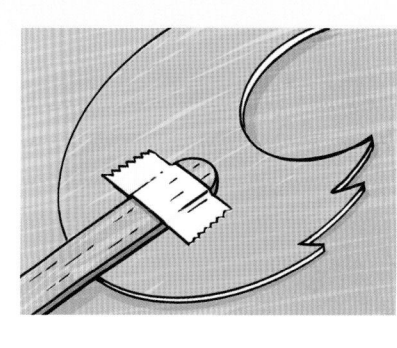

4 Firmly tape a craft stick or twig on the wrong side so you can peg your chicken in the ground.

11 Ears to you

Your Easter bunny card will really stick out from the rest!

You can also make the back of the bunny and glue it onto the back of the card.

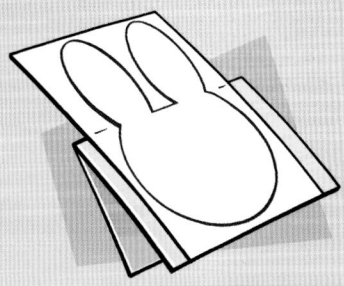

1 Take a piece of coloured card and a piece of white card, each 20cm x 15cm (or A5). Measure the halfway point of the coloured card and make a tiny mark each side. Fold.

2 On the white card, draw a rabbit with the base of the ears roughly level with the marks.

3 Cut out your rabbit and glue it on the folded card. Use a marker pen or cut-outs for the rabbit's face and whiskers.

Send your card unfolded to protect the ears. They will stick up when the card is folded.

12 Woolly sheep

Newborn lambs are a traditional symbol of Easter. One reason is that Jesus described himself as a good shepherd, and those who follow his teaching as his flock.

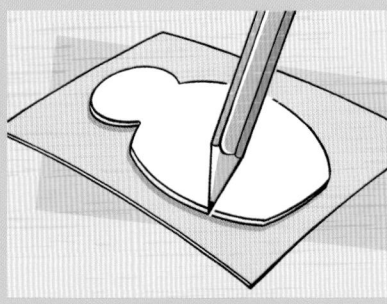

1 Copy the sheep shape shown below or draw your own. Use it to cut a sheep shape in stout card, or two thinner pieces you then glue together.

2 Paint the sheep shape both sides with gesso. Leave to dry. It may help to press the card flat under a heavy book overnight.

3 Paint two clothes pegs. Then paint the sheep's head.

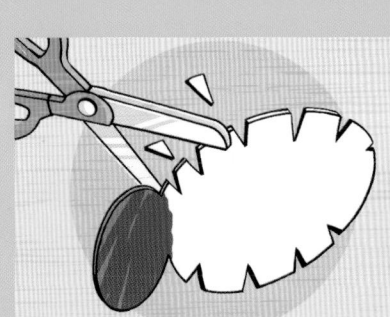

4 Make snips about 15mm apart all round the body, avoiding the head and where the legs join.

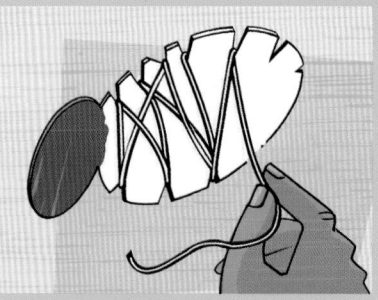

5 Now tape some fleecy wool to the back of the sheep and begin winding, taking care to catch the wool in a snip with each turn. Tuck the end under.

Add peg legs to make your sheep stand up.

13 Easter vase

Make the most of Eastertime flowers by giving a posy that includes a vase made from a glass jar.

1 Choose a small jar that goes in a little at the "neck". You can check this by seeing if there is a place where a rubber band sits snugly.

2 Using a large plate as a guide, cut 2 or 3 circles from green tissue paper or green cellophane. The diameter of the plate should be about 4 times the height of the jar.

3 Fold each circle in half and half again and cut leaf-shaped dips as shown.

Just a few flowers will look pretty in their paper greenery. Add ribbon or raffia to hide the rubber band.

4 Unfold the circles and arrange them one on top the other. Then centre the jar on them and gather up the circles to wrap the jar as shown.

5 While you hold the wrapping, ask a helper to slip a rubber band over the base of the jar and fit it at the neck. Rearrange the folds.

14 Chocolate nests

These egg-filled nests are the simplest. More complicated nests are for the birds!

Ask a grown-up before you do any cooking, and wash your hands.

1 Mix together 150g crushed Shredded Wheat and 200g finely crushed gingernuts. You can begin by breaking these into a plastic bag and crushing them with the end of a rolling pin.

2 Put 100g butter, 100g dark chocolate, and 2 tablespoons of golden syrup in a bowl. Ask a grown-up to melt the ingredients in a microwave, then pour the liquid into the cereal mix. Stir.

3 Line a muffin tin with paper cases and spoon some of the mix into each. Use a teaspoon to make a hollow in each one, then chill until set.

Fill your nests with tiny chocolate eggs or jelly beans.

15 Easter basket

This quick-to-make Easter basket is a stylish way to give a large egg, a clutch of eggs… or a bunch of flowers.

 The painting can be messy. Be sure to protect your working area with scrap paper, and wear an apron.

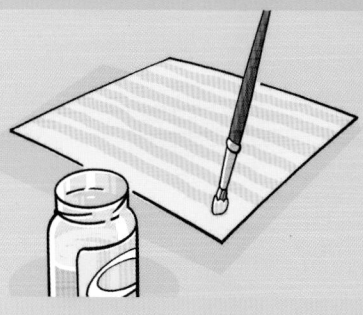

1 Take a piece of coloured card and paint stripes in a matching colour.

2 When the paint is just dry, paint stripes crossways.

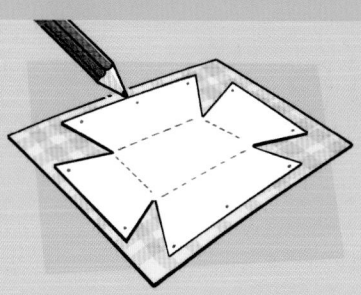

3 Copy the template on the back cover onto paper and cut it out. Use it to mark the shape onto thin card. Mark the place where the holes should go.

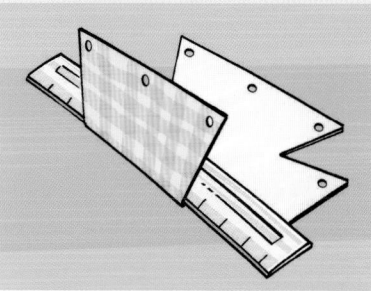

4 Cut out the shape and punch the holes. Use a ruler to help make the creases so the sides stand up from the base.

5 Thread ribbon or raffia through pairs of corner holes to make the sides. Tie in another piece for the handle, knotting each end so they can't slip through the hole.

16 Fingerprint chicks

You can print loads of these chirpy characters and then give each one its own personality.

1 Put yellow paint on a plate. Dip in a finger, blot, and print.

2 Add details when the paint is dry.

Try making an Easter poster or cards using the fingerprint chicks.

Happy Easter!